TWAYNE'S WORLD AUTHORS SERIES

A Survey of the World's Literature

Sylvia E. Bowman, Indiana University

GENERAL EDITOR

GREECE

Mary P. Gianos, Detroit Institute of Technology

EDITOR

Aristotle

(TWAS 211)

TWAYNE'S WORLD AUTHORS SERIES (TWAS)

The purpose of TWAS is to survey the major writers —novelists, dramatists, historians, poets, philosophers, and critics—of the nations of the world. Among the national literatures covered are those of Australia, Canada, China, Eastern Europe, France, Germany, Greece, India, Italy, Japan, Latin America, the Netherlands, New Zealand, Poland, Russia, Scandinavia, Spain, and the African nations, as well as Hebrew, Yiddish, and Latin Classical literatures. This survey is complemented by Twayne's United States Authors Series and English Authors Series.

The intent of each volume in these series is to present a critical-analytical study of the works of the writer; to include biographical and historical material that may be necessary for understanding, appreciation, and critical appraisal of the writer; and to present all material in clear, concise English—but not to vitiate the scholarly content of the work by doing so.

Aristotle

By JOHN FERGUSON

The Open University

Twayne Publishers, Inc. :: New York

In Piam Memoriam
C.F.A.

Introduction

"Inability to philosophise would render a scholar incompetent to grasp Aristotle's ideas, of which he would be likely to give a philosophically too easy, as well as merely external, account." So said Miss Anscombe, salutarily. The converse may also be true. Philosophy has become so technical that ability to philosophize may also be a barrier to the true understanding of an ancient Greek. When Lady Heath edited her husband's *Mathematics in Aristotle* she confessed that she had thought Aristotle for specialists only, but she warmed to her task with increasing interest and enthusiasm. I find myself, like A. E. Housman on a celebrated occasion, "betwixt and between," aware of Miss Anscombe's warning and that she and others may find this essay superficial, yet feeling that it would be disastrous if no attempt were made to help the general reader through Aristotle.

For this is the sole object of this book. It might be entitled, after Paul Shorey's well-known book on Plato, *What Aristotle Said*. If it has a merit, that merit is comprehensiveness. There are other introductions to Aristotle, some of them excellent, and some in their arrangement by topics no doubt clearer in expounding the main lines of Aristotle's thought. This is primarily an introduction to Aristotle's writings, and I have attempted as comprehensive a coverage as possible. Inevitably this has not left room for critical discussion of controversial interpretations. Some of these I have frankly evaded; on others I have taken a more dogmatic stand than I feel or put without argument a view which in other circumstances might be defended at length. Basically, I have been following Aristotle's text. I have read across the years and reread recently a good deal of Aristotelian criticism, but not more than a fraction of the whole; it will not be difficult to find articles which I ought to know and don't; and any scholar can ride his pet hobbyhorse over some part of this interpretation. If it clarifies some points for some readers, enables students who have to concentrate on a book or two to see them in context, and above all sends new readers to Aristotle himself, I shall be more than satisfied.

Acknowledgments

Gratitude is due to Oxford University Press for the use of the quotation from D'Arcy Thompson's *Science and the Classics* in chapter five, and to Mrs. Elna Lucas and the Hogarth Press for the use of the quotation from F. L. Lucas's *Tragedy* in chapter nine.

I have a number of debts to acknowledge. First to Prof. Mary P. Gianos, editor of the Twayne Greek Series, for her friendship and encouragement. Then to Prof. David Balme, whose movement from West Africa to Queen Mary College, London, oddly inverted my own, and whose brilliant lectures as a young don at Cambridge first made Aristotle exciting for me. At the same period I was grateful to the clear exposition of the future Sir Desmond Lee, and was fortunate to be confronted with the personal teaching and influence of one of the greatest of all Cambridge teachers, Rev. C. F. Angus. Anyone, especially in Britain, writing on Aristotle, can hardly fail to have absorbed the work of Sir David Ross, consciously or unconsciously, and, though I knew him only slightly, I have been greatly influenced by his writings. The manuscript itself has been exposed to the ministrations of two kindly critics, one an expert, my friend and colleague, Prof. Godfrey Vesey, the other a layman, my wife. My mother, Mrs. Nesta Ferguson, D.Sc., has checked the chapter on biology. Theirs is the credit for clarification and accuracy, mine the guilt for remanent error and infelicity. Further thanks are due to my wife for the index. Finally, a succession of secretaries have reduced my illegibilities to typescript and made the rough places plain—Mrs. Norma Steele, Miss Greta Cerasale, and Mrs. Sheila Beaney; Miss Lesley Roff has checked the proofs. To them special gratitude is due.

J. F.

Contents

CHAPTER 1

Life and Times

ARISTOTLE was born in 384 B.C.; his birthplace was Stagira, the modern Stavro, on the northern coast of the Aegean; his father, Nicomachus, was a doctor; his parents died before he was grown-up, and he was brought up by a guardian named Proxenus. In these four statements is contained virtually all that we know of Aristotle's most formative years, and each is significant.

For the first, Aristotle is a child of the uncertainties prevalent in the Greek world of the fourth century. By a combination of geography and temperament, Greek life depended on the *polis*, the city-state, a limited area centering on an urban capital. Each area was compact enough for direct government by the citizens— adult, male, and indigenous; the difference between oligarchy and democracy was in degree rather than in kind, depending on the extension of power through the lowering of a property-qualification. Across the centuries we can trace a general pattern of political development, from monarchy through aristocracy through dictatorship to democracy, but many of the cities became arrested at one of the earlier stages, and often there was a seesaw between the rich and the poor. Each city-state was jealously independent, and they did not find it easy to act in concert. To the east lay the massive monarchy of Persia, to the south Egypt slumbered in the dotage of its glory. Then at the beginning of the fifth century the Greeks achieved a measure of cohesion in driving back the onset of Persia. A wave of optimism surged up, especially at Athens, which, following the work begun by the dictator Pisistratus in the sixth century, now was firmly established as a major cultural center, and which by sea power established a series of alliances around the Aegean and beyond that too easily turned into an empire. Athenian economic power challenged Corinth, especially when it moved westward; Athenian political power challenged Sparta. In 431 an uneasy truce broke into open war, and the war dragged on, hot or cold, for twenty-seven years—that is, nearly twice as long as the Second Punic War, nearly five times as long as the Second World War, and nearly seven times as long as the First World War. Aristotle was born into a postwar situation. The parallels with more recent postwar situations are just, because human nature does not essentially change. The older generation wanted to carry on as if nothing had happened; there were young idealists growing up during the war who hoped to build something better; and gradually there emerged a new generation, which cared little for the past. For the moment the old formula of the city-state continued. One city after another came to some military and political dominance: first, Sparta, the victors in the war; then, with extraordinary resilience, Athens; and after, through the military and personal genius of Epaminondas, Thebes. But the formula was outplayed, and those who discerned the signs of the times saw that there was no future except in unity. At Athens Isocrates pleaded for the free adoption of such unity, and when his eloquence was admired but unheeded, he turned to seek a monarch as the point of unity. We are confronted with an age uncertain of itself and of where it is going.

Secondly, Aristotle was born out of the main current of Greek affairs, as it must have seemed at the time. Stagira was, however, firmly Greek, and Georges Méautis, a fervent Platonist, was talking nonsense when he described Aristotle as a semibarbarian, suggesting that the soul of Greece was a closed book to him. Yet Aristotle, Greek as he was, retained a certain detachment from the Greek world, which helped to sustain his scientific objectivity. He came to Athens in particular as an expatriate, a resident alien, on a visitor's visa, as it were. His enemies twitted him with his independence, his dapper neatness, and his enjoyment of the good things of life; he remained somehow alien in appearance and habit. But his birth at Stagira had another consequence. Over to the west lay Pella, capital of the kingdom of Macedon. At the turn of the century, shortly before Aristotle's birth, a monarch named Archelaus had taken steps to modernize his realm. Economically, he had adopted the Persian coin standard, developed the internal road system, developed contacts by sea through his new capital at Pella not far from the coast, and fostered trade. Militarily, he had reorganized his armed forces, strengthened his country's defenses, and introduced systematic military training. Culturally, he had attracted to his court some of the leading figures of the day, the musician Timotheus, the dramatist Euripides, the historian Thucydides, and others. Aristotle had an awareness of and sympathy for Macedon beyond those of most Greeks of his time. Its political stability contrasted with the chaos farther south, and its mood of progress offered something not obviously available elsewhere.

Thirdly, Aristotle's father was a doctor, a member of the guild of the Asclepiadae. The philosophic tradition in Greece was limited in its use of scientific method. There was a steady elimination of supernatural intervention in favor of natural causation. There was a sensible use of analogy from the natural world; this is strong in Empedocles. There was some observation; Democritus was a careful observer of nature. There was an astonishing faculty for systematic speculation. But there was little concept of the patient collection of facts and observations till they fall into a pattern or theory, and the subsequent testing of that pattern or theory by additional observation or experiment. In Cornford's celebrated example, Empedocles believed that we breathe through the pores of our chest; he did not think to insert himself up to the neck in a bath of water to test his theory. But among the Hippocratic doctors on the island of Cos we find real science, notably in the collection of forty-two case histories, carefully observed and succinctly recorded, with no attempts at prognosis or diagnosis, a document from which, when sufficient observations had been made, generalizations might be derived. That Aristotle was brought up in this discipline we may be certain; medical analogy is too prominent in his work to allow us to think otherwise. Further, he had some introduction to practical skills, notably dissection; there is evidence in his written work of some fifty dissections. It seems likely that there was some connection between the study of medicine and the study of biology, to which he later made such notable contributions.

Fourthly, there is his position as an orphan. There was something odd about Aristotle's psychology. He did not follow through his obvious career as a doctor, and we do not know how he spent his time between his father's death and his arrival at the Academy. Later he declared that a gentleman should have medical knowledge but should not stoop to medical practice. This suggests an underlying contempt for his father, and an attitude of superiority, a rejection of his father. It is evident that when he came to

Athens Plato became a father-figure to him. There is a touching story, which may be anecdotal but which is certainly *ben trovato*, that Plato gave a public reading of *Phaedo*, and his audience melted away before the difficult argumentation till only Aristotle was left. Yet here too his position was ambivalent, and we are conscious of a kind of spiritual Oedipus complex in his rejection of his teacher's most cherished views; "he kicked me away" said Plato later, "like a colt its mother."

He arrived in Athens in 367 to study with Plato. How he heard of Plato and what the precise attraction the sixty-year-old teacher had for him we do not know. The situation was anomalous: Plato was absent in Sicily at the time of Aristotle's arrival; it is hard to say what difference this made to the impressionable young man beyond building up his expectations. For twenty years he remained a member of Plato's Academy, and this was the first formative period of his advanced thought. It was a period of uneasy politics. At Leuctra in 371, Thebes had achieved some kind of hegemony, which lasted until the death of Epaminondas at Mantinea nine years later. Athenian ambitions were resurgent, but her new alliance broke up in 357; there followed an era of bourgeois prosperity under the skilled financial leadership and practical pacifism of Eubulus. Meanwhile, Philip II had come to power at Pella in 359, welded together a powerful professional army, built up a considerable economic empire, and used his superb diplomatic skill to extend his power with a minimum of dangerous conflict.

These events will not have passed Aristotle by, for the Academy was a training ground for practical politics. But the Academy stood for something very different from what those words suggest; to understand this, we must swiftly survey the development of Greek philosophy. It happens that our chief, though not our only source for this, is Aristotle himself, and his evidence has been seriously called in question; it is alleged that he read his own presuppositions back into his predecessors. It is my view that this skepticism is overstated and that his evidence is basically reliable. Somewhere in the early sixth century the Greek cities of Asia Minor showed a quickening of intellectual activity. We may speculate on the causes: the crosscurrents of culture, the economic effect of the new coinage, the power released by the development of alphabetic script, the transition from shame-culture to guilt-culture, and the new individualism.

Thales of Miletus and his successors asked questions about the fundamental constitution of the material world, and were not content with mythological answers. What is the basic constituent of the cosmos? Water? Or air? Or fire? Or none of these, but a substance indefinable in our experience? And how does a single substance change to produce the varied diversity of the world we know? The answers came and went, and in the early fifth century two thinkers of contrary genius brought the matter to a seeming impasse. Parmenides carried logical speculation to its extreme. All one can say of the universe is that it is. To admit change is to bring non-existence into existence, for change is the coming into existence of that which did not exist before. Change is therefore an illusion. Parmenides's ratiocination was backed by the subtle paradoxes of Zeno of Elea showing the apparent impossibility of motion.

The shadow of Parmenides hung over Greek thought for a full century; Aristotle was still seeking to disperse it. On the other hand Heraclitus and his followers argued that the material world is in a continual flux. "You cannot step into the same river twice," said Heraclitus, for the waters are always flowing past, and it is not the same river, and his disciple Cratylus argued that by the same token you cannot step into the same river once, since it is meaningless to speak of the same river. Heraclitus admitted a principle of stability or balance, and some kind of rationale behind the universe, but the very principle of tension between opposing forces implies that the world is a complex of such forces. On the one hand there is the impossibility of change, on the other the universality of change; it is a pretty contradiction, and we know that Plato studied with professors of both schools.

The physical speculators were not daunted. There was no future in monism; they turned to pluralism. First, Empedocles proposed not one "root" but four—earth, air, fire, and water—with forces of attraction and repulsion, which he called Love and Strife, to unite and part them. Then Anaxagoras offered a more complex scheme. Interpretation is controversial, but it seems that he regarded the substances of our world, flesh, hair, gold, bread, and the like, as infinitely divisible, yet each containing portions of everything else in a kind of chemical fusion. From this it was a short step to the full atomism of Leucippus and Democritus. These were late in diffusion. Democritus came from Abdera on the outskirts of Thrace, and only wrote *The Lesser World Order* in 405. Plato shows no trace of knowledge of atomism before *The Sophist*. Aristotle, however, is closely aware of Democritus. He must always have been an omnivorous reader, and it is possible that he introduced his views to the Academy.

Meanwhile, there was another strand in the pattern. In the middle of the fifth century the demand for education, not least to enable citizens to play a more effective rôle in democratic politics, had thrown up a group of teachers called Sophists. It was they who performed the office, which Cicero later attributed to Socrates, of bringing Philosophy down from the sky and settling her on earth; they turned from the macrocosm to the microcosm and abandoned cosmology for more practical subjects. Their general mood was skeptical about things ultimate, and they tended to a wide-ranging versatility, which was commendable provided that it avoided superficiality. The best of them, men like Protagoras and Thrasymachus, had genuine scholarship, and made serious contributions to literary criticism and to mathematics, to name two fields only. At Athens Socrates (469–399) seemed to fall into this pattern. He had started as a scientific investigator, but had become increasingly absorbed by ethical and political questions. Unlike the other Sophists he did not demand fees; indeed he claimed not to teach, and used leading questions to expose a too easy assumption of knowledge in the arrogant and to draw out the inherent potentialities of the more modest. Socrates was seeking ethical definitions; he was not content with the enumeration of examples of, say, courage or justice or piety, but was seeking "courage-in-itself," the thing which, inherent in all acts of courage, gives them their quality of courage.

Plato (427–347) was an aristocrat with literary, political, and intellectual leanings. The influence of Socrates led him to abandon the writing of drama as such, though formidable literary and dramatic gifts are in evidence in his philosophic writings. Politically, he was expecting to make his mark. But the excesses of the oligarchy that came to power at Athens after the war and contained relatives of his, and the execution of Socrates by the restored democracy, led him to despair of the actual political scene;

ten years of meditation on these events led him to his famous view
that mankind would never be rightly governed until philosophers
became kings and kings philosophers. In the meantime, he was
writing a reasonably authentic record of the sort of ethical dialogue in which Socrates engaged. At the back of his mind was a
nagging worry about the impossibility of reconciling the Parmeni-
dean and Heraclitean world views.

In 387 Plato visited Sicily and Italy. There he encountered the
Pythagoreans, with their almost monastic communities, their political involvement, and their curious combination of mysticism
and mathematics. He was just forty, a late age for an initial major
discovery. Everything suddenly fitted into place for him. He
returned to Athens and wrote *Phaedo,* an elaboration of the
scene at Socrates's deathbed, in which Socrates's concern for the
health of the soul and his cool agnosticism about the future ex-
plode at the touch of Pythagoras into the certainty of immortality.
Further, contact with Pythagorean mathematics gave Plato the
notion of an ideal world, which this material world imperfectly
reflects, just as we may make statements about "the circle" (as
that the angle subtended by the diameter at any point of the cir-
cumference is a right angle), which are never more than approxi-
mately true of any visible circle, but which are absolutely true of
circularity. So came the celebrated Theory of Forms or Ideas. The
world we perceive with the senses is relative, changing, fluctuat-
ing, impermanent. Behind it lies the true world, absolute, static,
permanent, apprehended by the intellect, the world of Forms. So
Plato reconciled the views of Heraclitus, which left nothing in a
state of being and everything in a state of becoming, with those of
Parmenides, which left nothing in a state of becoming and everything in a state of being, by his theory of two worlds, though it
will be noted that he did not thereby really solve Parmenides's
problem. Further, by "separating the Forms" he provided an answer to Socrates's search for ethical definitions in offering a tran-
scendent norm of behavior. The Pythagoreans also gave him the
idea of what we should call a residential university for the training of statesmen, in the park called the Academy. Socrates's use of
dialogue was formalized into dialectic, and the search for defini-
tion by induction and analysis was a regular discipline. We may
assume from *The Republic* that mathematics was used to lift the
mind to the eternal verities, the true statesman will try to incorpo-

rate in his politics; there will have been a deal of discussion of ethics and politics and Plato's ideal state, dissected by Aristotle many years later. This was the world which Aristotle entered.

He was a brilliant student. Plato nicknamed him "The Brain," and said that where others needed the spur he needed the rein. But his arrival coincided with a crisis in the Academy. Plato had an invitation to implement some of his theories of political education at Syracuse. It was impossible to refuse, and, given the actual situation, impossible to succeed. The experience was traumatic, and when Plato turned next to write about politics his views are embittered and authoritarian. Further, it is clear that about the time of his return, the Theory of Forms was subjected to a whole series of cogent criticisms, which led Plato to weighty modifications without destroying his faith in the theory itself. Plato presented these criticisms in his *Parmenides*. They are closely similar to those which Aristotle later offered. Now in all his numerous citations from Plato's writings, Aristotle never mentions *Parmenides*. It is difficult to resist the conclusion that the reason is that they are his own criticisms. So we get this picture of a smooth, brilliant, arrogant young man encountering Plato's theories in Plato's absence, fascinated by the Master's intellectual personality, daring to challenge him, and pressing his challenge, and receiving a partial answer that partially satisfies him for the moment, with an injunction not to think quite so hard.

In 348, Philip sacked Olynthus, and there was an anti-Macedonian outburst in Athens; we may imagine Aristotle keeping within doors, and bound to Athens only by Plato's old age. When Plato died in the following year, the property in the Academy stayed within the family and passed to his nephew Speusippus. Aristotle's main tie was broken. He may have felt slighted not to be Plato's successor; he may have felt that his continued presence might embarrass Speusippus; he may indeed have already left in the disturbances of the previous year. At the age of thirty-seven, after twenty sedentary years, he set out on the move, first to Assos in Asia Minor at the invitation of Hermeias (one of Plato's more successful political disciples), whose ward Pythias he married, and then to the island of Lesbos, where his friend and colleague Theophrastus lived. An examination of the place-names in his *History of Animals* has shown how this period was formative to his whole work in biology; over a third of the references are to Asia

Minor, and if we add Macedon and the Troad it accounts for nearly half; further, of thirty-eight references to places in northwest Asia Minor, fourteen refer to Lesbos, and no less than six to the lagoon at Pyrrha. It is as a marine biologist that Aristotle stands supreme, and it is likely that Assos, Mitylene, and Pyrrha provided his main opportunities for these researches.

In 342, Aristotle accepted Philip's invitation to tutor the fourteen-year-old Alexander. Any intensive tutelage can hardly have lasted more than one or two years, since from 340 Alexander was heavily occupied with affairs of state. There is little evidence of any deep influence. Politically, Aristotle looked to the past, Alexander to the future; and there is irony in the spectacle of the man who was to write that the non-Greek is by nature a slave tutoring the boy who was to admit the Persians to partnership in his empire. Aristotle had perforce to turn to literary studies, and he produced an edition of *The Iliad* for his teaching purposes. He returned to some of the political questions on which he had sharpened his mind in the Academy, and perhaps now conceived the idea of applying to political science the methods of biological science, the slow, patient, detached, accurate compilation of fact before generalizations are made; however, this did not prevent him from writing monographs on *Monarchy* and *Colonies*. He also continued his biological research. Aristotle was in Macedon during the dominance of the unscrupulous ambition and eloquent parochialism of Demosthenes at Athens, and the failure of his policies before Philip's military power.

Philip was murdered in 336. Alexander succeeded, and was well beyond tutelage. He secured the Balkans and crushed resistance in Greece, then in 334 crossed into Asia and in a series of breathless campaigns and heroic adventures changed the face of the world. Suddenly, the horizons had been flung back. With rare exceptions the thinkers of the past had been local, tribal in their scope; the thinkers of the age that followed would take the world as their parish. The city-state was dead until it could find its place as a municipality with limited self-government within a wider unit.

In this revolution Aristotle had no part. He now returned to Athens. Xenocrates had taken over the Academy; Aristotle set up a rival college at the Lyceum by the Ilissus where Socrates liked to walk. Here there were shrines to Apollo and to the Muses. Aris-

totle rented these and other buildings, including a covered walk
(which gave to the college the name Peripatetic). Here he established the first of the great libraries, a collection of maps, and a
natural history museum. Alexander offered to keep him supplied
with specimens from the more distant parts of Asia, but if these
ever came they were too late for examination in his biological
treatises. Here Aristotle lived a communal life with his colleagues
and research students. These were years of immense labor and
energy. Almost all the surviving works belong to this period, and
behind these, apart altogether from their originality of thought,
lay a vast cooperative effort in the accumulation of source material. A small example is by its very nature illuminating: he and his
nephew Callisthenes compiled a list of victors in the Pythian
games. The surviving works are memoranda or lecture notes
from which Aristotle actually lectured. Some few parts are in im-
pressively elegant and powerful Greek; such passages are to be
found in *Ethics 10, Parts of Animals 1,* and *Metaphysics 12.* For
the most part the writing is crabbed and bare. C. F. Angus, a well-
known Cambridge teacher who read widely and wrote little, once
told me that he was reading Greek and excerpting in Greek what
he was reading: he discovered that the style of his notes was a
close approximation to Aristotle's.

In 323 Alexander died. Demosthenes's party was cock-a-whoop.
Anti-Macedonian feeling surged up. Aristotle, with the fate of Socrates in mind, withdrew to the pro-Macedonian stronghold of
Chalcis in Euboea, as he put it with some wit, "to save the Athe-
nians from sinning a second time against philosophy," leaving his
friend Theophrastus, another scholar of exceptional distinction, in
charge of the Lyceum. At Chalcis he died of a disease of the di-
gestive organs, leaving behind him a thoughtful and affectionate
will.

CHAPTER 2

The Lost Dialogues

TO those who have labored through the surviving work of Aristotle it is a shock to be confronted with the critical judgment of Cicero, who spoke of the "golden stream of his rhetoric" or Quintilian, who appraised "the smooth charm of his style." [1] They were referring to a considerable output of polished literary work in the form of dialogues, written largely during his period at the Academy under the influence of Plato. But the Plato Aristotle knew had lost the dramatic power of his earlier writing, and was tending more to continuous exposition with occasional murmurs of approval from the supposed participants than to a genuine meeting of minds in dialogue; and this was the pattern Aristotle and Cicero after him used. The Platonic influence is seen in the very titles: *The Dinner-Party, The Sophist, The Statesman, Menexenus, Justice* (perhaps the original title of book I of *The Republic*), *Pleasure* (a suitable subtitle for Plato's *Philebus*). Most of these are no more than names to us; we may add *The Poets, Wealth, Prayer, Good Birth, Education, The Lover and Nerinthus.* One of the earliest works honored Grylus, Xenophon's son who died at Mantinea in 362–361. This may safely be dated to about 360; its theme was rhetoric, and it was related to Plato's *Gorgias* as assuredly as if it had borne that name.

But what was the relation? The question is a knotty one. That the dialogues embodied a different philosophy from that of the treatises may be taken as certain: once the treatises were rediscovered they largely replaced the dialogues in the attention of the Peripatetic philosophers, and Alexander of Aphrodisias, a man who combined learning and intelligence, was constrained to the hypothesis that the dialogues presented the opinions of others. This was a saner interpretation than the suggestion that the published (or exoteric) discourses are to be contrasted with views, which were not only unpublished but esoteric, a kind of mystical revelation to a closed fraternity; of this there is no trace in truth.

But if the Peripatetics neglected the dialogues, the Neo-Platonists seized on them as an authentic expression of Platonism. There are two other cogent pieces of evidence of their Platonic content. There is an interesting passage in Eusebius (*PE*, 14, 6), derived from Numenius, which tells how one of Isocrates's students named Cephisodorus was anxious to rebut Aristotle's criticisms of Isocrates. He did not know Aristotle personally, but thinking him an exponent of Plato's philosophy, he used this as a weapon against him. We may suppose (unlike Eusebius) that Cephisodorus knew what he was doing. Further, Plutarch speaks, with apparent reference to the dialogues, of "Aristotle's Platonic works" (*Col.* 20). The evidence might seem unequivocal; yet we find ourselves asking, if these are Platonic, what was Aristotle doing in reduplicating works that Plato had already written. However, there is contradictory evidence. Plutarch, in the same work, and Proclus later, quote plainly from the same source, a passage from the dialogues (fr. 8) to the effect that he could not go along with the Theory of Forms, even if he should be accused of disagreeing for the sake of disagreement. It is likely that this is the only passage where the disagreement is so explicit, but it leads us to suppose that the clever young man was not afraid to try to go one better than Plato in his presentation of subjects that Plato had already treated. We shall not go far wrong if we see the early dialogues as the work of an already original but still immature mind starting from the standpoint of Plato, but not afraid to be critical.

Three of these works call for rather fuller treatment, even if we recognize that our reconstruction must be speculative.

I "Eudemus"

The first is *Eudemus*. Eudemus was a Cypriot friend of Aristotle. He died in 354–353, and the dialogue in his honor was written shortly after; its natural model is *Phaedo*. But it was no pale imitation, for it too dealt with a real person and a real situation. Eudemus, in banishment, fell ill in Thessaly; he was given up by the doctors. But in a dream a handsome young man told him that he would recover, that the dictator of Pherae would shortly fall, and that Eudemus would return home five years later. The first two prophecies were fulfilled. Five years later Eudemus fell fighting at Syracuse; he returned not to Cyprus but to his true home. This was Aristotle's text; and he told the story as an introduction. The work is of the genre called Consolations, rather than a systematic philosophical exposition. But it contains philosophy. A long passage in *Phaedo* deals with the view that the soul is a state of being in tune, an epiphenomenon, which disappears when its instrument falls apart. Plato's refutation is long, cumbersome, and not particularly persuasive. Aristotle treated the problem syllogistically: "Being in tune has a contrary, namely being out of tune. But the soul has no contrary therefore the soul is not the state of being in tune"; it is an anticipation of the doctrine later formulated in *The Categories,* that substance admits no contrary. A second argument is presented more elaborately, but it is essentially simple. An out-of-tune body is an ignoble body. But ignoble men have souls. Therefore, the soul is not a state of being in tune. The passage seems typical of the dialogues. We are dealing with the themes that Plato treated and that start from his broad presuppositions, but the treatment is sharpened and refined. A second subtheme sees a more revolutionary change. Aristotle evidently claimed that the soul, before birth and after death, perceived "souls, forms and spiritual beings" (fr. 11). There is no problem about this as it stands, for even if Plato did not explicitly in *Phaedo* write of the soul's perception of Forms after death, it is in full accord with his general thought. But a close scrutiny suggests that Aristotle may be setting soul among the Forms. This is exactly what he is doing (fr. 8), and he is doing it in Plato's sense of Form, not in that of his own later doctrine. There is nothing of this in *Phaedo,* and at first blink it seems not to accord with Plato's teaching. But to Plato the Forms alone are perfectly real, and if soul is not found there, soul is not perfectly real, and that which is perfectly real is without soul, without life. Plato makes the point in *The Sophist* and modifies his theory accordingly, so that Aristotle is incorporating, if not inaugurating, a change of thinking in the Academy. The dialogue ended, like *Phaedo,* with a myth, a myth of Mictas and Silenus (fr. 44). Silenus says, "It is absolutely impossible for men to grasp the supreme good; they cannot share in the nature of perfection. For the supreme good for all men and women is not to be born. But if they are born, the best—and men can reach this—is to die as quickly as possible." To be born is to enter what Plato called the

world of becoming. The words are the same; it is to leave the
world of being. This is a brilliant adaptation of the sort of popular
saw that we find in tragedy to a genuine philosophic consolation.
The soul's true home is not here.

II   "The Exhortation to Philosophy"

Protrepticus,[2] or better, *The Exhortation to Philosophy*, was a
work of considerable influence. Thus it was the starting point for
Cicero's lost *Hortensius*, and it was extensively used by the Neo-
platonist Iamblichus in compiling his own *Protrepticus*. Iamblichus is our chief source in reconstructing Aristotle's original, and
this creates problems since it is difficult to be certain what is Iamblichus and what is Aristotle. Aristotle's work was dedicated to a
Cypriot baron named Themiso. Somewhere in the mid-350s Isocrates published his *Antidosis*, a defense of the educational proce-
dures of his college. The two colleges were rivals, and a compari-
son suggests either that Isocrates is answering Aristotle, or that
Aristotle is presenting a defense of education in the Academy in
response to Isocrates's claims.

As in other works of this period, Aristotle starts from a Platonic
model, in this instance *Euthydemus*, but his treatment of his subject is exceptionally free. The aim of the work, to challenge a ruler
to be a philosopher, is Platonic; and so is its content. The presentation is Aristotle's. As in *Eudemus* he cut through the knots of
argument with a pithy syllogistic presentation: "You assert that
philosophy is a 'must'; then philosophy is a 'must.' You deny
that philosophy is a 'must'; then philosophy is a 'must.' Either way
philosophy is a 'must' " (fr. 51). He means of course that philosophy is needed to disprove the necessity of philosophy. The main
tenets of *Protrepticus* are that intellectual wisdom is the crown of
the virtues, and that happiness rests in the health of the soul. Four
famous illustrations appeared in the course of his argument. He
showed that in the Isles of the Blessed all the other virtues would
be left behind; there would be nothing except the intellectual life
and philosophic contemplation; and it would be foolish to be confronted with a bliss, which we had not prepared ourselves to
enjoy (fr. 58).

Another passage claims that it is foolish to spend effort and risk
danger in sailing to the Pillars of Heracles (the Straits of Gibral-
tar) in pursuit of wealth, and to make no comparable effort in

pursuit of intellectual wisdom (fr. 52). Another excellent illustration is taken from the legendary Lynceus with the X-ray eyes (as we would say) (fr. 59). Imagine him looking at a handsome body, at a man with the pride of reputation in his looks, a television star, an Alcibiades, and peering through the outer trappings to the true man. The outer trappings are so transient; this, together with our folly, is why we cling to them. Lynceus reminds us to strive for what is lasting. A powerful image expresses the relation of soul to body. Etruscan pirates used to shackle their prisoners to a putrefying corpse; so the soul in durance to the body is in punishment and torment till it be freed (fr. 60). These illustrations reveal a sensitive thinker and powerful writer. The philosophy is still Plato's. The true philosopher deals not in copies but in originals; he contemplates things-in-themselves. But this study is also supremely relevant to practical politics, which admits of what we might call a mathematically exact approach. This view differs from Aristotle's later empirical and pragmatic approach, but it is sheer Platonism. The true statesman is not a manipulator or operator; he fixes his mind on the eternal verities and seeks that the scene on earth shall reflect them as fully as possible. Finally, we may note that the whole work is infused with the strong dualism represented by the last illustration. The soul's home is not here, but we have a taste of the divine in the faculty of reason. This leads Aristotle to his conclusion: "This being so, we ought either to pursue philosophy or to have done with life and leave the world, since everything else is empty verbiage" (fr. 61).

III *A History of Philosophy*

A third early work which we can discuss fruitfully was simply entitled *Philosophy*. It is later than the other two; Aristotle has begun to move decisively away from Plato; and it is hard to say whether this work belongs to the period immediately before or immediately after he left Athens. It seems that he made himself the central speaker; he was presenting a philosophy that had affinities with the later Plato but was nonetheless detached. The work was in three books, and each was in a sense self-contained, rather as Cicero divided his philosophic writings. In the first book we feel that we are meeting for the first time the real Aristotle, the scientist who bases his generalizations upon a careful compilation of fact. It offered something of a history of philosophy, viewed not

in isolation from religion but as part of a single system of development. It began from the Magi, and spoke of the Orphics, the
Seven Sages, and the wisdom of Delphi. The importance of this
treatment is threefold. First, we have a critical examination of
philosophic traditions, and an attempt to establish a sound historical framework for the study of philosophy.

Second, Plato takes his place in historical context, and the place
is an exalted one, since Aristotle espouses a cyclical view and sees
Plato following Zoroaster as a peak of the cycle. Third, the bringing together of religion and philosophy is in a curious way a half-
way house between metaphysics and science. Aristotle accepts
enthusiastically the doctrine of the divinity of the stars, and this is
part of his turning away from the invisible forms to the solid reality of the visible world. It also gives him a Platonic base from
which to criticize Plato, for the second book contained a systematic rejection of Plato's Theory of Forms. The Platonists had come
to identify Forms with Numbers; Aristotle explicitly rejected this
(fr. 9). He was now ready to stand on his own feet. In the third
book he offered his own world view. We may here concentrate on
five points in his exposition. First, we find a characteristically
concise demonstration of the existence of God; it is a form of the
ontological argument: "Where there is a better, there must be a
best; among existing things one is better than another; therefore
there is a best, which must be the divine" (fr. 16). Second, along-
side this we find an affirmation of what Otto has taught us to see
as the essence of religion, the numinous, *das Heilige,* Kant's "ever-
increasing awe."

Third, Aristotle's picture of God is not yet clear: he has not
worked out a systematic theology and he uses language loosely,
sometimes speaking of God as pure intellect, sometimes as the
universe, sometimes as the aether, sometimes as a kind of power
behind the universe; the thought is close to the post-Platonic
Epinomis in its vague religiosity. Fourth, the doctrine that the
stars are divine is carefully argued. Finally, we may cite at length
one remarkable passage (fr. 12).

"Imagine a race of men who had always lived underground in fine
luxurious homes decorated with statues and pictures and all the
luxurious trappings millionaires enjoy. Imagine that they had
never emerged on the earth's surface, but had heard at second

hand of a divine presence and power. Imagine that the jaws of the earth suddenly opened and released them into the world in which we live. When they suddenly saw earth, sea and sky, when they grasped the extent of the clouds and the strength of the winds, when they set eyes on the sun in all his glory and grandeur diffusing his beams to produce our day, above all when night laid darkness on the earth and they perceived the whole expanse of the sky studded with stars, the varying phases of the moon, the rising and setting of the constellations and their immutably fixed courses—faced with these spectacles would they not draw the conclusion that gods do exist and these things are their handiwork?"

It is a notable passage. It starts from Plato, for its model is the simile of the cave in *The Republic*. But its purport is totally different. Plato is using an analogy of the type used in *A Romance of Flatland:* as the material world stands to the shadows in the cave, so stands the world of Forms to the material world. However, Aristotle all but stops in the glory and wonder of the material world. His thinking is now poles apart from that of Plato.

Yet he started from Plato. The Aristotle of this period has never been better characterized than by Jaeger: "The old controversy whether Aristotle understood Plato shows a complete lack of comprehension. He appears to stand upon the same ground and wrestle with Plato for better insight; but his victory consists not in refuting him but in impressing the stamp of his own nature on everything Platonic that he touches." [3]

IV "The Theology of Aristotle"

Almost all that we write about the lost dialogues is in part speculative, and we may reasonably conclude with an additional speculation. The great period of Arabic philosophy was deeply indebted to Aristotle. But the Arabs were also affected by a curious work called *The Theology of Aristotle,* and the stimulus to their intellectual effort came not merely from reconciling Aristotle with *the Qu'rān,* but from reconciling this work with the authentic works which they also knew. For *The Theology of Aristotle* is a neo-Platonic compilation, and does not express mature Aristotelianism, except in two brief paragraphs which summarize some of the teaching of *Physics* and *Metaphysics.* For the rest it presents what appears at first sight to be a blend of Aristotle with Neo-Platonism.

It treats the Divine Sovereignty, as the cause and originator of causes, the cause of motion without being moved, and the way in which "the luminous force steals from it over mind, and through the medium of mind, over nature, and from soul, through the medium of nature, over the things that come to be and pass away." [4] It goes on to the splendor of the intelligible world and its divine forms, which are reflected in the material world, where multiplicity prevents the appearance of full reality. Next it treats the universal celestial soul, the beauty of the stars, the sublunary sphere, and the influence of the celestial power within it; the descent and ascent of reasoning souls and vegetable souls, the soul of the earth and of fire, and much else besides. It has been generally assumed that the Neo-Platonists were imposing their own philosophy on Aristotle. But we know from other sources that the Neo-Platonists found in the dialogues matter more acceptable to their own views than the treatises offered, and drew freely on them; this is only to be expected, since Aristotle was closer to Plato at that period. One wonders, therefore, whether the author of *The Theology of Aristotle* was not drawing on the dialogues, and whether this summary may not be a clue to some of the contents of the dialogues— even to the Unmoved Mover, about which Aristotle was not wholly consistent.

CHAPTER 3

Logic

I *Logic as a Tool to Learning*

ARISTOTLE created the science of logic: this is simple historical fact. It was not for him one of the branches of learning—theoretical, practical, or productive—but an instrument that all must use to reach true conclusions. His commentator, Alexander of Aphrodisias, was right in calling logic an *organon* or tool, and since the sixth century A.D. the word has been used as a general name for the logical treatises.

Two short works preface the collection. The first is usually called *Categories*;[1] it is an analysis of terms. Aristotle's list of categories, with his examples, is as follows (lb25):

SUBSTANCE:	man, horse
HOW LARGE:	two cubits long, three cubits long
OF WHAT KIND:	white, literate
IN RELATION TO SOMETHING:	double, half, larger
WHERE:	in the Lyceum, in the city-center
WHEN:	yesterday, last year
BEING IN A POSITION:	is lying down, is sitting
BEING IN A STATE:	is wearing shoes, is wearing arms
ACTING:	is cutting, is burning
BEING ACTED ON:	is being cut, is being burned

The word *categoria* means predicate. All these may be predicated of some subject; it is a list of modes of being. Aristotle lists the basic questions which can be asked about anything, with his eye (as the eighth shows) on human beings. He offers a protection against fallacy caused by the similar linguistic form of different predications. The result is an embryonic theory of type of distinctions. When he repeats the list in *Topics* (103b23) he replaces substance with WHAT IS IT. The list is neither doctrinaire nor

definitive: elsewhere he omits position and state; but some such
list as a tool for analysis is taken for granted in most of his works.
We may note that it is a tool of limited applicability: it does not
help us to analyze all propositions or to define all subjects. It over-
stresses the proposition that is formed of subject plus predicate, a
limitation, which hampered the development of logic down to the
time of Leibniz. Even within its own limits it can be sharpened:
we would wish to divide HOW LARGE between number and
extension. But Aristotle is scrupulously careful not to claim too
much for it; it is a technique, not a metaphysical analysis. It seems
to have been original with him. It is not to be found in the Academy, which was busy with ontological analysis of a different kind,
though Plato's work in *The Sophist* was his starting point. It may
have been devised in answer to the logical quibbles of some of the
contemporary Socratic schools:[2] "Socrates is white; white is not
Socrates; therefore Socrates is not Socrates."

It is however surprising to find substance[3] treated as a predicate, since substance is that of which other things are predicated.
The explanation is that for Aristotle substance has a double mean-
ing. It is true that "a substance in the most authoritative, primary
and strict sense" is "that which is not asserted of a subject, and
does not inhere in a subject, e.g., a particular man, a particular
horse," that which Aristotle likes to call "a *this*" (2a11). But there
is also a secondary sense of substance, to mean species or genus,
such as "man" or "animal." Socrates is an example of primary substance; Socrates is not to be predicated of any other subject. But
"Socrates is a man" and "Socrates is an animal" are normal and
natural descriptive sentences, and must find a place in *Categories*.
It will be noticed that though Aristotle's analysis is in general linguistic, in his distinction between primary and secondary substance we see the scientist, preoccupied with the solid reality of
individual physical data, rebuking his metaphysical mentor Plato,
yet retaining an element of Platonism. The last sections of *Categories* are not by Aristotle.

II   "On Interpretation"

The other preliminary work, *On Interpretation,* passes from
terms to propositions, from uncombined terms to combined terms.
A sentence, in its simplest form noun plus verb, is significant
speech, of which each part is meaningful as well as the whole

(16b26). All sentences are meaningful; but only propositions contain truth or falsity; a prayer is an example of a sentence that cannot be called true or false. The simplest form of proposition affirms or denies one thing or another, in past, present, or future. Propositions, affirmative and negative, may be universal, individual, or partial (particular), e.g., all men are white; Socrates is white; some men are white; Socrates is not white; some men are not white. Traditional logic, however, came to treat individual propositions as special cases of universal propositions: "All Socrateses are white" where the set contains only one term. In the Middle Ages it became convenient to allude to the four basic forms of proposition by vowels derived from the Latin words *AffIrmo* (I affirm) and *nEgO* (I deny), so that A = universal affirmative, I = partial affirmative, E = universal negative, and O = partial negative. Aristotle also analyses sentences under the heading of modality, distinguishing between assertorial, apodeictic, and problematic propositions: "X belongs to Y," "X necessarily belongs to Y," "X may possibly belong to Y."

Aristotle makes an important distinction between contradictory and contrary. Two propositions are contradictory when the one asserts or denies the whole of what the other asserts or denies in part: of two contradictory propositions one must be true, one false. O is the contradictory of A, I is the contradictory of E; "some men are white," "no man is white" are contradictions. Two propositions are contrary when they stand in direct opposition; and both may be false. A and E are contraries; and unless one is an extreme pessimist or an extreme optimist, the contrary propositions, "All men are liars" and "No man is a liar," are both false. Aristotle is aware of the relationship later called subcontrary. I and O are subcontrary: both can be true, but both cannot be false. The full implications of this were worked out in the Middle Ages in the so-called square of opposition.

This is implicit rather than explicit in Aristotle. We may conveniently here add a word on "conversion" of propositions, which he treats at the beginning of *Prior Analytics* (25a1). Some propositions convert; that is to say, a valid proposition can be formed from a given proposition with the order of the terms reversed. One of the commonest fallacies in popular thought arises from assuming that simple conversion applies. If every pleasure is good, it does not follow that every good is a pleasure, only that some good things are pleasures: A converts to I. Simple conversion applies only to E and I: if no Cretan is a truthteller, it follows that no truthteller is a Cretan; and if some Texans are boasters, then some boasters are Texans. O does not convert.

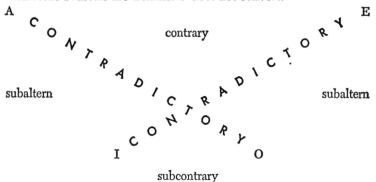

A   contrary   E

subaltern   subaltern

I   O
                              subcontrary

Behind all this lies a correspondence theory of truth. At the outset of *On Interpretation* Aristotle speaks of words as symbols or signs of something that is happening inside the speaker. Words may vary in different languages, but the inner experiences they represent are the same for all, and those experiences are likenesses of objective realities, which are the same for all (16a4). Concepts are the likenesses of things. Propositions combine or separate them. A proposition is true or false if there is a correspondence between the combination or separation of concepts and the combination or separation of the things they represent. It is interesting to compare this with the words of the great British empirical philosopher John Locke: "Truth, then, seems to me, in the proper import of the word, to signify nothing but the *joining or separating of Signs,* as *the Things signified by them do agree or disagree with one another.* The joining or separating of signs here meant, is what by another name we call *proposition.* So that truth properly belongs only to propositions: whereof there are two sorts, viz., mental and verbal; as there are two sorts of signs commonly made use of, viz., ideas and words." [4]

III   *The Syllogism*

With *Prior Analytics* we are introduced to Aristotle's greatest contribution to logic, the syllogism. "A syllogism is a form of